SELFLESS LOVE

WOMEN AND NATURE

AF578659

BALBIR SINGH

Copyright © Balbir Singh
All Rights Reserved.

This book has been self-published with all reasonable efforts taken to make the material error-free by the author. No part of this book shall be used, reproduced in any manner whatsoever without written permission from the author, except in the case of brief quotations embodied in critical articles and reviews.

The Author of this book is solely responsible and liable for its content including but not limited to the views, representations, descriptions, statements, information, opinions and references ["Content"]. The Content of this book shall not constitute or be construed or deemed to reflect the opinion or expression of the Publisher or Editor. Neither the Publisher nor Editor endorse or approve the Content of this book or guarantee the reliability, accuracy or completeness of the Content published herein and do not make any representations or warranties of any kind, express or implied, including but not limited to the implied warranties of merchantability, fitness for a particular purpose. The Publisher and Editor shall not be liable whatsoever for any errors, omissions, whether such errors or omissions result from negligence, accident, or any other cause or claims for loss or damages of any kind, including without limitation, indirect or consequential loss or damage arising out of use, inability to use, or about the reliability, accuracy or sufficiency of the information contained in this book.

Made with ♥ on the Notion Press Platform
www.notionpress.com

Contents

Contents

Preface

POET'S WORDS

The journey of writing poems started since 1998 (college time) when I was pursuing my Master degree in English Literature. First poem " Smoke in the Dense Woods" was written incidentally. While sitting in the college ground saw a smoke rising from amongst the dense forest of Bijli Mahadev hill. Impressed by"Beauty and Love of Nature" initially, included the theme "Beauty and love for Women", later, for it came to me that both Nature and women can be replaced for each-other. Both possesses same qualities and attributes. Both nurtures and provides substances and care to others. Both possesses stunning beauty. Both are resilient. Both have unbelievable abilities to adjust to changing circumstances and recognising the value of relationships and community. This relationship reflected in "A Honeybee and Two Roses" and many other poems. Both are connected to all living things and operates on cycles in terms of growth, transformation and renewal. Yet, in spite of these subltelities both are being exploited and trodden by the man's selfishness and greed.

A deep and self-less love has been manifested through " Self-less love", " A Gift of Nature" etc. not to be mistaken by sensual, physical, and bodily desires. All the poems expresses pure, spiritual and passionless love for Nature and its live counterpart i.e. Woman.

In this Journey many poems have been written but maximum of these have lost as I used to write and throw them somewhere in my cupboard or under the bed sheet. I wish this "Selfless Love" reach people's mind with whatever work left me through this publication.

Balbir

1. SMOKE IN THE DENSE WOODS

Introduction: Daytime saw a cloud of smoke rising from the dense forest o Bijli Mahadev Hill from college ground. Same mid-night my sleep was disturbed and tossed a lot in the bed to go to sleep but couldn't. The scene emerges in mind at mid night and given the form of a poem.

Far among the dense-woods
Gusting out the smoke,
Sometime heavy, sometime slow;
Appears ghastly flow.
Sometime seems a saint dwelling
Under the Oak,
And sometime as thick cloud
Emerging from mysterious snow.

Advancing in fixed direction
As if guided by spirit,
To meet a companion,

To hail and greet,
Lost in the dense woods,
Having longings so sweet.

A lovely savage place,
No man can dare
To go without courage,
Bore in this world by rare.
He must have, sure,
All tools for care
But wonder is that
How he managed living there?

2. Self-less Love

Introduction: While pursuing my B.ed. from Education college Dharamshala, one saw a beautiful girl studying in Degree college and emotions poured like this:

Lips like rose, eyes like lake,
Hard to say going shine whose fate.
Elf, fairy, above Hellen of Troy;
No one in the world is at par to you.

Shining face is serene, calm and smooth (Natural)
On seeing this shame with feel the moon.
Smile as if blossoming of beautiful flowers
Speaking as if season of attractive, sweet showers.

Silky, fragranced and sweet scented hair,
Floating carelessly as if Wind-God taking all care.
Graceful, charming and poised walking,
As if waves of ocean rising and falling.

In sea of beauty I have dived very deep,
Its upon you, let me die or keep.
Only a glimpse will serve the purpose for me
Have mercy, Nymph, nothing else I wish from thee.

3. A Cuckoo (Part-I)

Introduction: I appreciates beauty very much and love beautiful things. Wish everyone should be happy and if see anyone in grief, tries to please him to utmost.

When the beautiful Spring comes,
A Cuckoo delighted feels,
His sweet voice enchants all,
So pleasant and soothing to soul.

When on lush green mango trees, Sweet songs it utters,
Then only lovely blossoms occurs.
If he ever forget to sit on, flowers do not peep out,
And remains under shutters.

From one to another,
Swiftly and softly, he flies,
Favourite halts are mango trees,
Rejoices as one of them he sees.

By nature tender at heart,
Couldn't dishearten anyone,
Flies and consoles at call-short,
Leave not until the pleasure done.

Whenever he saw anyone in grief,
At once he flies to it,
Sings so sweetly, so lovely,
Disbursed happiness, then only quit.

4. A Cuckoo (Part-2)

Once in a beautiful orchard,
Saw a pretty Mango tree,
Feels so attractive towards,
As its eyes full of hope, he see.

Sat on it for a while
Left not, as so sweet was smile,
Received so love and care,
To break that trust, he never dare.

It wants him to sing only,
For itself and not for others,
Feels dejected, as his nature
Was happiness on all to shower.

As in Autumn, Winter and Summer
You can see no swing,
It must realise the truth that
Cuckoo can sing when there is only Spring.

5. "EVERYTIME I TRIED TO CLOSE"

Every time I tried to close,
A Game Played by my fate,
She has gifted me those curses,
Noboby else as my mate.

Desire, as in everyone, for beauty
Flourished in my heart,
Initially, the response was at par,
Then a sudden thunderbolt broken tar.

She discoursed well and sweet,
Passion of love all increased,
What happened? What thunder?
That cleft heart; caused disaster?

I loved and respected,
She mocked and rejected,
With no fault in my love,
To unbearable pain, I was subjected.

I shall love, I shall respect,
Respond the way, you like,
Nobody's fault than myself,
May God bless, kindly, thyself.

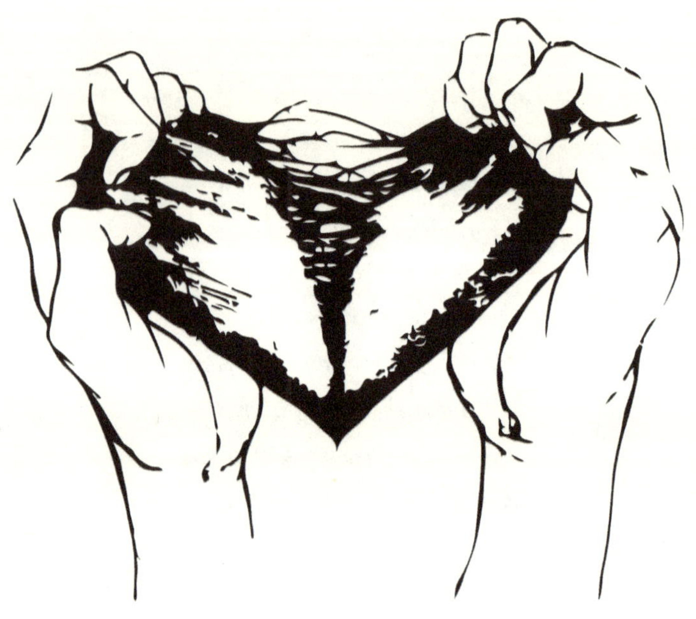

6. MRIDUL

You are a fairy came from heaven,
God has sent you to tease the heart of Man.
I like you very much
But can't declare to you
For you the Kohinoor
Rich than me must be in queue.

You can not be bargained,
Even for diamond and gold,
And value little even if
All my body and love sold.

You are heaven, I am earth,
Never meet though seems to meet,
For you it will matter nothing
Even if I lay my heart at your feet.

In this materialistic world
All is vain; to strive, to seek.
After return to God's paradise
Definitely "you and I" destined to meet.

7. "PURE AND INNOCENT"

Wandering aimlessly in this hopeless world,
He was heading but towards nothing.
One day soaring high in the desert sky
He senses Sweet honey-like fragrance smelling.

Curious to see the flower that was
Smelling so honey-like,
Somewhat excited and apprehensive,
To scented corner he made hesitated stride.

Flower was so delicate and beautiful,
Nothing in the world was at par,
Above Jasmine, Rose and Lotus,
First of its kind in whole world, I swear.

It was pure, innocent and sensitive
To save it from hardship, he became attentive,
Delicate wings spread in protection,
Wild shrug of it caused sharp dejection.
While in dejection, still wishing its welfare.....

8. "KANHA PRAY FOR YASHI : A LITTLE FAIRY"

A fairy has come from heaven,
For me she proven number 'Lucky seven',
Innocent and pure at heart though,
Peaceful and calm as 'piece of snow'.

God has blessed me with this little elf,
I must have done some benevolence, previous life,
I wish she flies high in this open sky,
My heart will be so glad to see her like.

When she learns her first flight,
Her tender wings will droop slight,
But with the help of Brother 'Kanha',
I am sure you touch the sky.

Yashi, must have some relation to Kanha,
Who prayed to God day and night.
"Please God! Send me from heaven", he says

A fairy with whom I can dance and play,

And this fairy in my house is result of of his pray.

9. HONEYBEE AND TWO ROSES

Once in a wonderful garden,
Full of plants and hedges,
There dwells two beautiful Roses,
Spreading sweet fragrances, sense arouses.

Fragrance and incense,
Everywhere and all around,
Apples and peach on the branches,
An attractive tiled path lay on the ground.

A visit by a Honeybee happens there by chances,
Flying beside and beneath the trees and hedges,
Fluttering and dancing in the sweet breeze
Felt mad to meet the conjuring incenses.

He gazed and gazed; searched and searched,
Eyes flashes the bushes inward,
The two beautiful roses he see,
Dancing on sparkling waves in glee.

Both were elegant,
Both were pretty,
At first sight he fell in love,
Want to have both in his settee.

Balancing the act of love and meeting,
As could't devote to both at the same time,
Hovering and sitting on one at a time,
Meeting and pleasing second other time.

Floating and flying high on the trees,
Never outsighting both from glance,
He used to please the sweet ones,
And they toss their heads in delightful dance.

Time evading ; the beauty fading,
Love of honey bee ever increasing,
Memory fills his heart with pleasure,
Even if got separated, will always be in seizure.

10. "FAITH"

Never doubt my faith
For God's sake,
Like a rock, like a cliff
My love and faith.

Neither silver nor gold
Nor diamond or any wealth of world,
Can bargain my faith, and
You think, in a market, it can be sold?

Never ever there is betray
Why then, your mind always stray,
All day long, Drone, after hovering high
At night, in flowers petals, come to stay.

Storms make the trees sway to and fro,
So many hustle-bustle or stirs, what so,
Without love, without trust, life has no sense,
Adopt the pace of 'Nature', her secret is 'Patience'.

faith

11. "BEAUTY"

All that glitters is not gold,
Everything in market, can't be sold,
Some faces in world may look beautiful,
Attractive; though in real sense no 'Beauty' hold.

Once in a beautiful place
I happen to meet an attractive face,
So alluring, so charming outside;
To discern, of benevolence there was no trace.

Beauty is empathy, beauty is soothing,
If one has more to say; beauty is in giving,
Tendering, caring and of compassion,
No sign could be found of generosity and altruism.

Beauty, kindness and fragrance like eternities,
All were missing in her dazzling light stall,
John Keats once said, "Beauty is truth, truth is beauty",
Nothing I could found in that sensual soul.

12. "A DAY IN SUMMER HILL VALLEY"

Tall, elegant and majestic,
There stands proud deodars trees,
Rising high across cool and clear creek,
Releasing life-giving and refreshing breeze.

Fine-textured and evergreen;
Ever-laughing and ever-ecstatic,
On either side erected and raised,
Concrete towers and life hectic.

The valley overstuffed and overloaded
With establishments and buildings called cities,
Once there must be standing proud trees,
Today destroyed by brutal activities.

Under I wish a solitude hut
Where nests mental peace,
Sparrow twitters, dove coos

And the parrots screech,
Have a farm down the creek
To satisfy bodily needs,
Does Nature have enough
To pacify unending human greeds?

13. "CHOTTI KASHI"

Narrow and broad lanes of this beautiful city
Crowded with traffic and loads
Of cars, two and three wheelers, buses and trucks,
And countless people hustling-bustling across roads.

Roadside stands selling in fruit and vegetables,
Variety stores dealing in daily needs, tables and cables,
Woodland, Addidas, Octeva, Bata with dazzling lights,
Can see footpath spread with local vegeis sights.

Baba Bhootnath, Mahamrityunjaya, Ekadasharudra;
Panchavaktra, Bhimakali and in Bhagwan Jagganath,
People have deep and incredible faith,
Hospitality and sweet-tone appeals to hearts straight.

Stunning and shining Indira Market in the middle,
Calm, serene, majestic, gorgeous 'Vyas' flowing by the side,
Raja Madhorai resides in the Rajmahal and,
Maa Sidhakali in the city and Maa Tarna on the Hillside.

Dhangsi in the east and Devdhar in the west,
In the east-south Kangni and Kehnwal in the south,

Uncertain Suketi flows in between and Paddal

The attraction of all sports loving youth.

Charming damsels can be seen in tusion
Strolling in the market in sensational fashion,
Tearing the heart of all ; young and old
Witnessing all, there stands the clock tower bold.

City is named 'Mandi' after rishi Mandavya,
Shivratri festival celebrated with faith, pomp and show,
Eighty one temples gives its name "Chhoti Kashi",
Famous 'Shiva Dham' after Kashi, where all people's heads bow.

14. "A Gift of Nature"

So radiant, so elating,
Is your smile,
So soothing, so subtle,
Can it ever be hostile?

Eyes like pools of beauty,
Want to swim to the depth,
So vast, so deep,
With unscalable length and bredth.

Lips like rosebuds,
Inviting and alluring,
My heart aches to
Hear gentle whispering.

Figure is a masterpiece,
None is near the stature,
Procelain, smooth and flawless,
A true marvel of Nature.

Hair just like a crown
Of glory and excellence,

Framing your sweet face
With grace and elegance.

Your presence is a gift,
A treasure to behold.
Radiance is above the
Diamond and gold.

Beauty emanates from within,
Just and licit,
A reflection of your kind
Heart and shining spirit.

15. A Gull in a Concrete Jungle

In the dense jungle of concretes,
There stands an elegant building,
Centre for activities of excellence,
Emerged through chartered streets.

Every great morning, when it shines
A group of sparrows,there, flocks,
Chittering-chattering all the day long
Flying back to their nests in evening.

By chance a Gull happens to pass by,
Came to an abrupt stop,
At that charming halt, by
The branchy, towered and poised top.

As jolly by nature He was.
The Gull used to sing, dance and Shrill.
Insane, lunatic, idiot thought by all
Lucid and discerning, by only one, still.

It was so pretty,
The beauty was not less
He feels enjoyed and delighted;
Thrilled and contented whenever sighted.

As Peacock dances when clouds hovers,
Used to dance whenever He saw it.
On pleasing and giving it happiness
Overwhelmed with mental peace.

Among its company did He feel
The joy of his desire.
Vital feelings of delights comes over
The spirit goes on hovering higher and higher.

16. "MOUSTACHE"

Moustache show proud
Voice is impressive and loud
What do you want? To hear me?
Don't want to come to near me?

Your vast chest
Is a place of my rest,
Your shining forehead and chin,
Want to kiss I really mean.

Your arms are so strong
You and I shall live together long
Life goes smoothly with a smile
We will go hand in hand in a style.

17. A HIMALAYAN RIVER

From the snow-capped peaks,
Through canyons and deep gorges,
Interlocking spurs and V-shaped valleys,
Burbling and gurgling You flows like cascades.

Gives life, provides habitats to earth's organisms,
Generates energy and source of great adventures,
Carving deep gorges flowing through lush valleys ,
And drains to shape the prosperous, fertile plains.

Heals wordly pain and purifying to soul,
Teaches our mind the sense of peace and control,
Remove obstacles, never stop and keep flowing; message it hail,
So that you ever remain fresh and do not slale.

18. FOUR SEASONS

As awakes the Spring
Petals make pop,
Then little birds sing
On newly green top.

Spring passes Summer comes
With his fire fall,
Sweating under the arms
Burning the soul.

To cool it down
Rainy showers comes,
From city to town
Relieving the pain.

Depressed Winter comes behind
Sharing his own sorrow,
No person can be found
Nothing to lend or borrow.

19. MIND

What is it, Over our shoulders ?
Storage house for ideas,emotions and beliefs,
Power beyond imagination if you notice,
A box full of tools to drive the novice.

No matter adverse the circumstances,
It's toughness can win all matches,
Sometimes discontented, other in bliss,
And sometime learn lesson from reminisce.

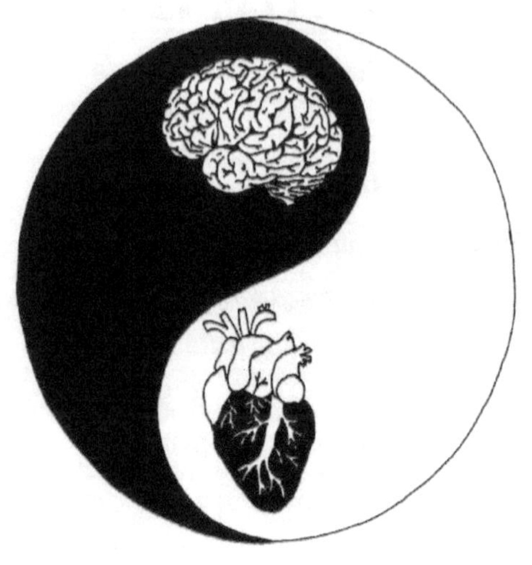

20. Travel through Forest

Way between the woods Of Maples,
High to the sky and stable,
Traveling through dark and dense,
Felt amazed at first glance.

On cedar and pine a silvered Frost,
Walked all way yet became lost,
Till it reached to a solitary place,
Where someone bade farewell to a pretty face.

Covered peaks, green meadows, flowers all around,
Birds, animals and heavenly falls altogether found,
True beauty with blissful essence,
Comes from within showing presence.

Time goes by; some come, some go,
Time passes , all changes
some have gone, other will,
Yet it will remain pure and still.

Joy and sorrow are
Just day and night,

One moment near, another away a mile,

And sometime stays for a while.

Truth lies unstained like a lotus in a lake,
Lovely, elegant and straight,
Time is transient, so is life on earth,
Soul emerge pure when burns in world's hearth.

21. Mr. Winter

Here comes Mr.. Winter
In his bag with petty treasure,
Merry for the younger
Cold and ill for older.

For some it may be sad,
Keep lying in the bed,
For me its beginning,
Comes other day after evening.

22. Love and Life

When day ends sun at edge,
Redness around the sky,
How beautiful it was !
Gorge of my heart saying good bye.

Time is transient so our life; uncertain,
Keep the Hate away,
Only love to gain,
Be gentle, be kind
Live your life but not in vain.

23. INNOCENT MOUNTAINS

Standing high, solemn and proud,
Stubborn and ever tenacious,
Rising tall to heaven, do not waver,
No matter conditions so ferocious.

Silvery peaks, lush green valleys,
Deep canyons with pebbly-shingly rivers,
Forests decorates slopes and cliffs,
Salubrious and healing climate attracts to ridges.

Alpine meadows, coniferous forests,
Home to variety of animals and birds,
Adventures like trekking,skiing, rafting and skydiving,
Rich cultural heritage and simple life straggling and striving.

Though pure and innocent still,
Yet Their heart is being drilled,
Glaciers receding, ridges sliding,
Fragile but tough there they stand smiling.

24. Rofus Treepie

Black capped, long and stiff tailed,
Rofus Treepie to my balcony sailed,
On seeing, all family felt delighted,
My father said, "Since long I sighted."

Perched on Railing with loud krowii-kroo,
Made intentions clear with a clamaroo,
Want to eat wheat grains drying in the sun,
Every movement enjoyed while it was feuling its engine.

25. Primitive Nature

Through the dense pine woods
A narrow road goes by,
The nature is deeply soothing to eye,
On either sides of road calendulas smiling by.

Undergrowth so green and primitive
As never been trodden by,
Cool and calm breeze so peaceful to mind,
When softly and silently kissing cheeks pass by.

Tops shining brilliantly in the sun,
The shade is soothing to soul,
Under goes a road with zigzag holes,
Leads to a settlement where human strolls.

Beautiful place to dwell,
Peaceful climate as well,
Only disturbed by a sound
That human activity spell.

26. Life

What is life ?
Endless births, Endless deaths,
Material fulfillment in this world whole,
Or mysterious Journey undertaken by soul?

Sum of past and present,
Or hidden in future's hope?
Some say worldly pleasure,
Other stresses purification of soul.

I say it's perceiving the world
As devine presence that helms,
Kindness, compassion and love ,
Above and beyond physical realms.

BE
KIND.

27. OCHREA

That morning's first glimpse
Left my heart so gratified,
Her vibrant orange-green look
Enough to keep my eyes so wide.

Colours complimented body radiance,
Designs added a touch of elegance,
Combination was so captivative and
Outfit, granted an implausible confidence.

Ochrea looked beautiful and stunning,
Her energy and spirit awe-inspiring ,
Like an elegant and poised queen
Walking gracefully and my heart rocking.

www.ingramcontent.com/pod-product-compliance
Lightning Source LLC
La Vergne TN
LVHW090128160826
845673LV00015B/1115

* 9 7 9 8 8 9 6 1 0 1 8 9 5 *